THE
FUTURE
IS WATCHING

Thoughts from the Classroom

JACKSON REAP

Fulton Books, Inc.
Meadville, PA

Published by Fulton Books 2019

ISBN 978-1-64654-044-0 (paperback)
ISBN 978-1-64654-045-7 (digital)

Printed in the United States of America

CONTENTS

INTRODUCTION

Many books on teaching give instructional tools on how to prepare great lessons, implement effective collaboration strategies, or classroom management guidelines, etc. We'll touch on those things, but the primary focus is on the mental and emotional success of three groups of people: students, teachers, and parents. With public school as our backdrop, the three groups mentioned aren't the only ones who may benefit. Provided are universal principles that can be applied within any industry or individual pursuit. In the end, my desire is to inspire others to be the best version of themselves as possible so that children can have adequate role models to follow into the future. Each of the three groups mentioned has a vital role to play in both the successes and failures of students. If teachers and parents can come to an understanding of their role, responsibility, and influence, it'll give students a greater chance at success themselves. The following pages should shine light on the mind-sets of students while providing adults avenues to success inside and outside the classroom. Through various observations and experiences, the main objective is to arm each group with strategic and psychological weapons in order to gain victory in all areas of life.

Using the public school system as a tapestry, various scenarios regarding human behavior highlight how, as adults, often we're the ones falling short, not students. It's easy to blame the ineptitude of children who scream through hallways and talk back to their teachers, sometimes even vandalizing property in and outside school, but this shouldn't deter teachers into habitual negativity and complaining. The primary goal of teachers should be to guide the youth into the future, rising above pessimism and procrastination. Ultimately, the goal of this writing is for the reader to gain greater peace of mind that leads toward self-mastery—first for themselves, but eventually for those in their sphere of influence, mainly students. Peeking behind the veil of public school, various observations of students, parents, and teachers reveal common behavioral patterns that we all can fall prey to.

Teaching can be a rewarding profession if approached alongside a healthy perspective. Unfortunately, it can also be a trap of mediocrity where patterns of negativity blind individuals from greater parts of themselves. Without the proper perspective and a healthy approach to your career, it's nearly impossible to make a lasting impact. Mindsets, attitudes, and strategies are presented in hopes of parents and teachers changing for the betterment of themselves and the ones who are watching, students.

This book goes out to all the teachers out there hitting their heads against a brick wall year after year with the same hardheaded, blank-staring kids. It's also directed to parents or anyone who's seeking to better themselves and the world around them. So, parents, if you want to gain a new perspective of what goes on with your child at school, the following should provide insights into what it takes for them to be successful, as well as some of the pitfalls that students can succumb to. If your child struggles, meaning their grades are less than average or you're constantly receiving calls from teachers and principals about their behavior, please understand, this book was written to help you! The unfortunate problem with help, however, is before you can receive it, you must admit you need it. So how do you know if you do? Well, the above criteria should've spelled it out. However, if you're not a parent or even a teacher, the principles discussed can be applied to any individual seeking to become a better version of themselves.

TEACHING IS A CALLING?

Some say that "teaching is a calling." I hear it all the time. When teachers share with others what they do for a living, many respond with "Wow, that's great! You're truly a hero. Such a sacrifice! Teachers deserve so much more recognition, money, resources," etc. All that may be true, *for some*. Teaching is a calling for those that go the extra mile, get to work early, stay late, and offer tutoring any/every opportunity they can. Those are the ones that likely utilize their precious couple months off during the summer to plan lessons for the next school year. Their dedication, determination, and investment toward students is truly invaluable, and they deserve more credit—and money! Gifted with patience, empathy, and a keen eye for potential, these teachers may be the very ones who qualify for the "calling" category.

People arrive in education for various reasons. Some knew they wanted to teach since childhood, and they earned their degree in education. After getting their feet wet their first few years in the classroom, they're super proud and fulfilled in their calling. They caught their groove early and could very well be one of the ones to make a lasting impact. A goal might be to advance outside the classroom in pursuit of revolutionizing curriculums, adjusting outdated structures, or changing the course of their school or even district. Growth and ingenuity are necessary as society changes and certain leaders are needed that can propel the system forward. I tip my hat to those teachers and wish them the best. They deserve a few extra apples on their desk. But not the typical red ones that "Pete the Teacher's Pet" brings on Mondays. No, these are the extra special green delicious apples grown in Washington, DC. You know, those that are deposited into a bank!

Others view teaching as a short-term stop while they finish a graduate program. These teachers are generally dedicated to working hard and doing their very best. With the drive to pursue higher education, you can generally expect that they'll work hard while they're on the job, but they may not feel like the classroom is their long-term landing spot for their entire career.

Some simply do it for the extended time off during summer. They see it as a simple gig where they don't have to work as much as people in the "corporate world." They know they won't get rich, but hey, all the time off! Or it may be a safety net for individuals still searching for or don't really believe in a "calling."

The truth is, many teachers aren't waking up in the morning, excited about going to work. For a good number of them, their job is just like any other; a bleak necessity in order to pay the bills and maybe eke out a vacation during the summer. Some have the notion that it's a career where they can help serve the youth and mold the future of a nation. As exciting as that prospect is, reality has a way of presenting surprising little details that aren't typically included in the "vision." Like anything else, the idea of something is far different than the reality.

As motivating as molding a nation sounds, the classroom is where the grind must begin for every budding leader in education, and it isn't usually very glamorous. Teaching is a calling for some but, nonetheless, is still a job. The joy of seeing the light switch go on in students is what keeps teachers coming back, but those moments are just that—moments. The day-to-day routine of school brings constant challenges. Many teachers are burdened with limited resources, strict guidelines, and a lot of monotonous, frustrating, busy work. Things like: team meetings, mandated state test preparation and grading, etc., a checklist of do's and don'ts, mixed in with a lot of coffee, hormones, and—praise God—government holidays!

Teachers sometimes imagine that they'll grow wings lifting them far, far away from their classrooms and their students. Stresses can pile up, and they'll naturally feel the need to vent. If teachers loved their jobs, their "callings," then why do they long for summer break just as badly as their students? Why do they get out of the building on Fridays like it's a fire drill? Why? Because no matter what motivational posters are in the room, teaching in the public school system can be a frustrating grind.

So, regardless if you feel that teaching is your calling or not, let's walk through this process with some perspective. Whether you absolutely love your job, hate it, or are simply working for a paycheck, there are ways to improve, and even perfect, your craft. For the teacher who's alternatively certified or undecided, wants to be successful but isn't sure if they're in it for the long hall, or simply seeking a fresh perspective and a few tips, the following chapters should help teachers manage students and themselves. Maybe you'll even have few laughs. Let's begin.

Storms on the Horizon

August. After two months of R and R, the reality of another school year dawns. For some, it's an exciting time to make a fresh start. For others, it's the bleak reality of another year where struggle and stress gather on the shores of education. Either way, hopefully, fun was had over the summer, but back to the grindstone it is.

Schools open several days before students return, giving teachers the opportunity to settle in. Most set up their classrooms in hopes of striking a chord of positive hardworking vibes, shop for necessities like pencils, glue, tissues, etc., and might luck out in finding some new creative motivational posters. If they're really feeling frisky, they might even throw in an old couch and lamp in the back to make it "feel more like home."

As pencils are sharpened and bookshelves filled, posters on the walls whisper wise words of wisdom, intended for students, but a healthy reminder for teachers as well. Once classrooms come together, the curtains pull back and the last days of preparation come to an end. It's time to put the boat in the water and set sail. After a little prayer, meditation, or happy hour—whatever's needed—it's time. Bon voyage, here we go!

Once the school doors swing open, hopefully, it's smooth sailing for a good while, but tragically for many teachers, the honeymoon of the new school year can quickly come to an end. In fact, it may never have begun in the first place. On the positive end, the excitement of meeting new students, reuniting with coworkers, and the consistency of a nine-to-five schedule can be a comforting routine. Schedule creates a sense of stability, plus it's nice to have consistent interaction with other working adults. Oftentimes though, if one's not careful, the energy in starting another year can quickly morph into the annoyance of obligation.

The first few weeks of school typically are the smoothest, comparable to a commute to work where traffic is flowing and every light's green. Students are on their best behavior, there's not much back talk, and they're generally subservient to teachers' demands. But speed must increase when entering the highway of arithmetic and grammar, so you better get in the left lane if you want to keep up! A kind soul may wave you over, and you might even be early to work. All's good in the 'hood, akin to students doing their work with a smile! No problems. However, the longer you're on the road, the more likely there'll be construction, or an accident that causes a backup that seemingly lasts forever.

These jams usually happen a few weeks into the year. If someone mindlessly cuts you off, you might be able to look past it, but then, when you're two miles from your destination, there's a wreck! Students stop doing their homework, or even the simple classwork that's assigned. Attitudes flare where chaos and destruction block the next intersection, causing a quarter mile back up. Now you're forced to take an alternate route, adding another fifteen minutes. The peaceful ride abruptly shifts to road rage. What do you do? How do you react? What's your first move once the traffic clears?

It takes character to keep your cool, on the road or in the classroom. Rising above students' negative behavior is one of the biggest struggles of teaching. Teachers should remind themselves when students get off track and start acting a fool, that they're simply *going through*. It's called puberty. They're not grown yet. Stay patient. If their foolishness is a little beyond typical childish/adolescent behavior, the last thing you should do is take it personally! Crude, rude, and with an attitude, they're simply revealing an aspect of their struggles they face outside the classroom. Remember, it probably has nothing to do with you. When this is understood, you've got a fighting chance.

Teachers, especially inexperienced ones, are sometimes just trying to find their way and navigate their course load. But the subject material is the least of a teacher's worries. Behavior management is where some of the most difficult challenges lie. With up to hundreds of children under a teacher's care each day, you can guarantee that at some point in the year, chaos will ensue. When—not if, but when—this happens, teachers must be prepared to prevent themselves from getting stressed or overwhelmed.

You must know you're walking into chaos when entering most schools. Surrounded by developing minds, hormonal hurricanes, and an avalanche of attitudes can drive the coolest of customers to the brink. Puberty/adolescence isn't pretty; it's not cute! It's annoying. There's nothing wrong with thinking that. It's the reality of the business teachers have chosen.

MOTIVATING STUDENTS

Don't you remember school growing up? If you're anything like me, you weren't thrilled with the freedom of summer getting snatched from you like a thief in the night! No more sleeping in, pool parties, and playing with friends. School brings with it forced responsibility, rules, and routines, not exactly a child's dream.

If there's anything for them to look forward to in August, it's reuniting with friends, sporting a new hairstyle or maybe showing off some new clothes. Most kids dread school. Math problems and science projects are the last thing they want to spend their time doing. There's much more important stuff for them to focus on. Things like Fortnite, Snapchat, Hot Cheetos, and of course, sleeping! The last day of summer is usually the worst day of their year. Shadows loom as they ponder alarm clocks beeping, homework assignments, and the demands of teachers' rules, which to them are seemingly pointless tasks. In many of their minds, they're looking at another nine-month sentence where school feels more like imprisonment than fun, so as a teacher, you're already starting out in a vulnerable position.

One of the most difficult challenges for teachers is motivating students to learn. Some kids, believe it or not, are excited about school. Teachers' Pets remain focused, assertive, responsible, and cooperative. Their summer reading was finished before the fireworks on the Fourth of July, and they eagerly anticipate filling their young minds with knowledge. These students generally can take care of themselves. They don't need to be redirected every few minutes, and you can trust that they'll follow directions without you sounding like a broken record. As they follow your lead into worlds of knowledge, the exchange between teacher and students make teaching a true joy. Typically, however, most children aren't interested and will begin veering off the path in due time. Teaching gifted and talented students is a breeze, but don't count on too many of those types sitting in your classes.

Convincing children that education is their doorway to success is difficult especially if they're lacking adequate examples of success at home. Most likely, if they don't understand the importance of education, whoever is responsible for guiding them at home doesn't either. If their parents aren't emphasizing the importance of education, or discussing concepts like authority, respect, etiquette, and honor, then students will likely believe one of the following:

A. Any type of authority is the enemy.
   or
B. All they need to do is work hard enough not to fail in order to get promoted to the next grade at the end of the year. (There's a crisis of illiterate high school graduates!)

These students are still reachable, if you're willing to accept the challenge. Children are easily influenced, and with a strong conviction and positive attitude, teachers have the power to shift the atmosphere and attitudes of their students. Teaching children/teenagers facts they're not interested in requires teachers to be determined to be positive. With the right mentality, you can shine light on their otherwise cloudy lives and inspire them to excel. If you can do that, you've accomplished a great feat!

One way to get through some of their mile-long stares is by looking at school from their perspective, which allows teachers to go on the offensive in preparation of what's before them. Getting into their mind-set is essential to understanding them so that you can communicate on their level. They often feel that teachers are these older, rude people who just give rules and demand they work hard but never take the time to get to know them.

Try to put yourself in their shoes. How would you feel about yourself if you were being taught, by you? Are you positive, funny, mean, boring, caring? What's your energy like? Are you inspiring or moping around like most students? Are your lessons more like a fruitcake (bland, tasteless, and last minute) or guacamole (exciting, delicious, and prepared with love)? If fruitcake is on the menu, it'll be like pulling teeth to get your students to eat.

Struggling students need someone to care enough about them to take the time to show them the way to success. This truly is a sacrifice. After long days in the classroom, trust me, it's no walk in the park. As professionals, we know what it takes to "make it" in life, or hopefully at the very least, pay our bills on time. We've graduated from college and have a career. Having grown up and earned our place, we have experiential knowledge of the real, adult world, which our students have yet to understand. With our life experience, we have simple expectations; things like: bringing supplies each day, completing assignments on time, or preparing for exams, etc.

When we come across students in seventh grade, for example, who rarely, if ever, bring supplies, are constantly tardy/absent, or are reading at or below an elementary school level, it's tempting to allow frustration to get the best of you. It's tough to hold these students' hands and give them your all, while also maintaining a positive attitude. Dismissing those students and categorizing them as a lost cause is common among teachers because the demands that they create can take their toll. They make the job much more difficult and tempt teachers to pull their own hair out at times, but they're also the ones who need us the most.

Read Between the Minds

The shock of schedules, homework, rules, and new routines initially takes the fight out of kids at the start of the year. Once students settle into their schedules, the back-to-school jitters slowly begin to wear off. Feeling more relaxed, their initial masks of insecurity fall by the wayside, and their true colors eventually shine.

It's interesting watching children with the freedom to express themselves. However, some students are more difficult to read and less willing to open up. Fear, insecurity, and anger create confusion as they search for their true north and who's on their side. Adolescence is the most awkward part of life. It's a time of transition from the innocence of childhood into the complexity of developing one's identity and all the thoughts and attitudes that come with it. Minds begin contemplating ideas and scenarios once never considered, things like body image, being "cool," and popularity rise to the forefront.

Growing up is difficult. Remember the awkwardness in your own experience? We're all trying to find our way, and children especially need direction. As bodies mature, physical changes confuse young minds unequipped for this new stage in their life. Puberty's a daunting experience for every child, that's for sure, but it's just as complex for the ones tasked with guarding and training them—parents and teachers.

Children, especially teens, want an answer to "why." Without proper guidance or a clear understanding of their direction in life, inquisitive kids can get frustrated. Overcome with boredom, they'll ask themselves why they're stuck at school. If no one's positively encouraging and challenging them, their idle minds will wander into dangerous territory and conjure up ideas based on whatever's there to fill the void: internet, media, music, friends, etc. (This could be *anything*!)

If children feel neglected or ignored and lacking guidance from strong adults in their life, they'll look for connection elsewhere for support, usually each other. This sadly becomes the blind leading the blind. People are social by nature. We're born with a desire for relationship and connection. Whether they realize it or not, students are starving for attention, acceptance, and guidance. If no one's giving them those things at home, then they'll be much more inclined to becoming stressed, anxious, or resentful during school. When confused kids find other like minds to play with, you're asking for trouble, double trouble. They'll feed off one another and create an even stronger compulsion to act out. Before you know it, the problem has compounded into a disaster.

As they say, birds of a feather flock together. The well-behaved and focused kids fly while the disenfranchised stumble along with other troublemakers. Neglected children, pending a miracle, will find other kids to hang out with who struggle with similar issues. "Neglected" doesn't have to be as extreme as not having food on the table or shoes that fit. It can be as minor as parents or teachers not truly listening. Many sensitive kids need a listening ear to feel loved and confidence is shattered when one feels alone in the world, especially in childhood.

What Is Smart?

There are two main types of smart in this world: street-smart and book-smart. A few blessed souls have both, but it's rare. Some students lack the test scores to show it, but they're very intelligent nonetheless. They're the street-smart who can read people and situations better than they can a textbook. These students are independent thinkers that look beyond the rules. They question authority, which isn't necessarily a bad thing; it's a sign of intelligence. But if you can't answer inquisitive questions, their respect and effort will likely go by the wayside. When parents or teachers can't accurately and lovingly answer their questions, the train will eventually teeter off the tracks.

Rebellion has many causes, one being a lack of guidance. Many rebellious kids are naturally intelligent but due to circumstances outside their control, they're lacking anyone to steer them in the right direction. Sometimes parents don't know how to control their child or flat out don't have the emotional ability to do so. They're so stressed or even negligent that they can hardly take care of themselves, much less a child. Unfortunately, many children are born into these types of situations where they're growing up without love or mentorship. So, teachers, be prepared with patience as you jump into your role as an authority. These types of students are the few who generally cause the most stress for teachers and administrators. They're not the majority, but it only takes one to spoil the bunch. Much attention must be made to this group because if not, they'll end up steering your ship.

While questioning the rules and the roles of teachers and administrators, they're quickly labeled *troublemakers* and get branded with the scarlet letter until they either graduate or, unfortunately, drop out. Threats, detentions, and even suspensions likely won't motivate them to change. Teachers don't like daydreamers that can't seem to pay attention. They're creative, outside-the-box thinkers that need to be approached with patience and care. I believe that many gifted, artistic, creative, and independent-thinking children often get prematurely diagnosed with learning disorders and are taught to feel that they have a problem when really, they may be an innovator who's bored and waiting for the right guidance! (Look at Albert Einstein!)

As grades go downhill, they'll likely become a distraction to their classmates and a major burden for teachers. They'll test their teachers to see exactly how much they can get away with. Anger and confusion build inside as they search for the answers to "why?" Why are they trapped in school? Why are these old farts making me do all this boring work?

Kids are looking for purpose. They want to know "what's the point of all this." If there's nobody at home helping them understand the complexities of life, rebellion quickly ensues. As children grow older, identity is most often prioritized over everything, especially grades. Kids want to figure out who they are, and who they should hang out with. They're searching for who's their crew. For many kids, that means experimentation and testing limits. Their potential for success is high, but their tendency for deviance is even greater. Confused and needing answers, they'll do what they can to see if you care or if you're just like "all the rest."

Children are also looking for stability, and if you show that you're shakable, you'll lose them. The trick is not to bite at their bark, or you'll lose the fight. Sometimes when children misbehave, they're looking to see if you'll crack at their foolishness. It's tempting to snap back at their snarky comments, but that's exactly what they want. They're going fishing to see if you'll take the bait. If you snap back with anger, they'll know that they've got you, and they'll continually push your buttons to cause a reaction. It's their pleasure and exactly what they're looking for. At this point, they'll have lost respect for you, making it much more difficult to gain it back.

When students aren't taught the importance of respect and honor at home, they'll eventually teeter off the tracks at school. Teachers expect students to know how to behave and show respect, but the reality is that many of them can't or flat out won't. The troublemakers, class clowns, and downright disrespectful bunch is the toughest to handle, but it's very possible that they can become your favorites in time, if you know how to reach them. They're desperate for attention, but their way of asking for it doesn't quite come with a polite smile, if you know what I mean.

On the other end of the spectrum are those that often get overlooked and are who I'll refer to as the "mice." They usually make little noise, appear small, and can disappear if you're not paying attention. Timid and reserved children are less inclined to act out but often try to stay invisible. Out of fear, they rarely ask for help and can remain hidden unless you consistently make a strong effort to engage them. Their fears and insecurities can outweigh their capacity to learn. Some of these students are so frightened from trauma that they're stuck in a shell, afraid to talk, ask questions, or express themselves. Most likely, they feel lost, neglected, misunderstood, or trapped by life. Both types, the rebellious and shy, are unknowingly crying for help, so how will you respond?

It's wise to keep a little rabbit in your hat with tricks to stay above the fray. Challenges always come a little easier with some secret knowledge and shortcuts to the destination. The secret is each difficulty you face provides with it a gift or a curse; that's up to you. Challenges always provide with them lessons if you're willing to do some digging. If you can find the lesson behind each "problem" you face, you'll ensure success for the next round.

TEACHERS

Teachers are a very peculiar group of people, cut from a different cloth, if you will. Going back to your time as a student, you must remember some teachers that were, kindly put, unique. Whether it was their crazy hair, giant belly, or awkward stain on their shirt, as a student you may have sensed that some of your teachers were a little different. Not all of them stuck out, many are quite normal people, but more than just a few probably still get talked about with old friends.

Having been in the profession for several years I've come across various personality types, teaching styles, attitudes, races, shapes, you name it. Regardless of your background or personality type, the following information provides some general ideas to consider before entering the classroom and, if followed, should hopefully make your experience a little smoother. If you're not a teacher, the principles discussed can be applied wherever you find yourself during your nine-to-five.

The first thing to consider is that the only thing you have control over in life is yourself. There are going to be other teachers and staff, including librarians, secretaries, administrators, lunch ladies, janitors and outside visitors at times (like parents), that can consistently get under your skin after a while. These same faces will cross your path regularly so remember the four walls of your classroom are your domain.

An important idea to surrender is the fantasy of a perfectly run school. It's not a teacher's job to manage the day-to-day logistics; that's the duty of secretaries and administrators. Teachers need to stay in their lane, master their craft, and allow others to focus on theirs. Remember, just like the rest of life, the only thing that you can control is yourself. When all your ducks are in a row, then you might be able to assist others on their journey. Do you, so you can help others too.

Wouldn't it be nice if instead of complaining about the stresses of our job we conquered, and rather than looking for others to blame, we looked at improving ourselves? The goal of this book is to provide teachers (and any working adult) with solutions to the seemingly endless amounts of difficulties faced each year. Hopefully, the following information will show one how to gain the strength necessary to pick up the falling students while pushing the ones already flying to even greater heights.

Prepare for Battle

Students stampeding through the hallways like the running of the bulls can be a common scene in many public schools. More impressive than the thundering herds of bodies frantically running to their next stable is the reality that after all the screaming urgency in getting to class on time, some of these little "bulls" are still tardy!

I love kids, individually or in small numbers. But when they get together in the hallways or are packed thirty plus to a classroom, it's an entirely different mountain to climb. Don't get me wrong; every day can bring some joy: like when the few students who always smile and are genuinely happy or when classes understand your lesson and seem enthusiastic about learning. Those times are great. But in between the sunshine, the clouds of nonsense can quickly gather. If chaos in the hallways doesn't irk you, your next masseuse appointment may be due to your students' constant disinterest in classwork.

As the school year progresses, attitudes begin to sprout, and the students' shining eager faces can seem to darken as quickly as a late fall afternoon. What was once "your calling" is now your job. Your "service" has become your obligation, and the countdown to Christmas begins, and it's only September!

If you're expecting children to walk into the classroom and automatically have respect for you simply because you're an adult or authority figure, well, that day has passed. Don't get me wrong, though. A lot of kids will happily comply with your demands, no questions asked. Most will, actually (depending on where you teach!). You can thank their parents or the school's structure for that. The kids who don't know or who haven't been taught what respect is are the most difficult challenges you'll face.

You must know what's coming your way. Be prepared for these little ninjas. Most won't show their true colors for at least a couple weeks. Unless you're a skilled detective, you probably won't be able to sniff out some of their devious tendencies until after they feel a little more comfortable.

A common mistake many teachers make is taking students' negative behavior personally. You must remember, unless you're being the jerk, they aren't acting out because of you. They most likely act that way with most of their other teachers or anyone else in authority. If they didn't do their homework or don't listen to the instructions in your class, it's not the first time they've done it, and it won't be the last. Don't get mad; don't react. Observe and take mental notes. Objectivity must overrule emotions if you're going to be victorious in this battle. When you find yourself consistently angry or bitter, the following should help:

First, be aware that you're angry. If you never get mad at a student, get short with them, or react with a snarky comment of your own, then tip of the hat to you, sir/ma'am! The rest of us mortals need to be reminded not to take things personally. Once you're aware that you're angry, the next step is to practice self-control. Your instinct may be to yell, criticize, or complain. You may even begin to neglect the hardworking and well-behaved students and start preaching to the annoying/disrespectful ones. As tempting as this may be, it's a disservice to the students who are actually eager to learn. If you find yourself continuously complaining, then you might end up digging yourself into an even deeper hole, losing even more of your students.

Creativity > Complaining

The complaint train is always accepting passengers, and if we choose to jump on board, the blame game can quickly pick up speed. With a full head of steam, we'll begin to believe that the problems we're facing are the faults of students, their parents, the administrators, or our colleagues. Right? It's important to remember when you're going through a difficult day that everyone else also has their own stresses and problems that they're dealing with.

It's common to resign yourself to the thought that students won't change. Teachers hope that the administrators and counselors will do a better job so that they can get back to focusing on teaching "good students." What a wonderful *fantasy*! The problem with this outlook is that teachers are the ones in the classroom every day.

Unfortunately, sometimes the help we want simply isn't available. Shifting the blame and making excuses, teachers will claim that it's not their fault anymore; rather, it's the administrators', because they just won't do anything to that little brat! Teachers love to say things like "He/she needs to be expelled! If I were the principal, I'd (insert fantasy). I'm doing everything I know to do, but no one takes my complaints seriously..." and on and on and on... Guess what? You're *not* the principal! No matter whose fault it is, it's *your* "problem" until the end of the year, so it might be wise to look for solutions rather than blame others who have their own issues to deal with.

The best thing you can do is to try to think of adjustments you could make that would help mediate the issues you may be facing. Unfortunately, for whatever reason, a lot of teachers never learn or are never taught how to deal with problem students. Managing a classroom filled with wandering minds takes its toll. If you dread the re-emergence of "the problem," please know that it's only a matter of time until that student feels the need to act out again. When—not if, but when—this happens, teachers often metaphorically (or literally) throw up their hands and scream for mercy.

Even after students receive appropriate discipline, it doesn't mean they'll change their behavior. Unless it's an extreme case where a child gets expelled, even if they get sent to an alternative school, the "bad apples" will come back to class after they've been warned for the umpteenth time, and they'll most likely continue to push their teachers' buttons. Without creative or productive ways in resolving conflicts, teachers oftentimes justify their own negativity. Problem students usually get the brunt of our energy, and after a while, if we're unable to get through to them, out of desperation, we'll look for help from administration.

After several hours or so of carousing kids, teachers need a break from all the hormones and may want to find some fellowship with other adults. Often, they'll take their frustrations to the teacher's lounge, and instead of decompressing, relaxing, and creatively looking for solutions, they'll spread their own negativity to other colleagues in hopes of finding some company for their misery. Ideally, the teacher's lounge would be a place where teachers come to let their hair down, relax, and regroup for the rest of the day. However, most of the time, it can often seem like a barn full of hens, cackling, complaining, and letting their frustrations fly.

It's easy to justify being angry and to complain. There's *a lot* to complain about, but it doesn't solve anything. It's akin to a dog barking at a tree. It's not going to change the situation—that tree (problem) ain't movin'. Whatever's going on, complaining is just wasted energy. Teachers constantly encounter situations where it may be appropriate, and their complaint skills are impeccable! Whether it's with their team or during department meetings, at home with the family (or cats) or out with friends, complaining or putting the blame on others for one's problems in life are natural and common reactions, but it accomplishes nothing. We need more teachers carrying a calm, confident and composed demeanor rather than headaches, complaints or gossip.

As a new teacher I would complain about the same things pretty much every evening after work, and I'd find myself constantly venting to my wife about a student, coworker, or administrator. I was used to and comfortable with venting, but I lacked any solutions. Overcome with stress, I'd just go on about my business and drag my feet, day after day. What I wasn't considering was how my attitude had an effect not only on myself and my experience, but on those around me, mainly my students. I was quick to point the finger but rarely took the time to consider my impact on the situation. After some intense soul-searching, I've found that the best remedy is pretty tough to swallow...

LOOK IN THE MIRROR

Before I was able to have real peace of mind, confidence, and the ability to maintain self-control, inside or outside of work, I had to take a slice of humble pie and start my search at an often-visited yet rarely critiqued spot: the mirror. I'm not talking about hairstyles or outfits; I'm referring to my attitude. I realized that I was the number one culprit for my negative experience! That's right, me! So what about you? Are you experiencing mostly frustration or joy at work? Do you find yourself complaining and looking for distractions to get through the day or thriving with creativity, eager to make an impact? If your experience in the classroom is anything like mine was—filled with stress, boredom or anxiety—then you may need to check yourself. Is it possible that you may be exhibiting the same negative behaviors as your problem students do?

What I've come to learn is that while teachers give instructions to children on simple subjects that we've technically mastered ourselves, students provide teachers a peek into their own psyche that can be a garden of wisdom if you allow it to be. The classroom will always bring with it the potential for chaos. The way you handle those times will reveal your level of resolve. Schools are a teaching ground for both a students' knowledge but also a teacher's ego.

I've learned far more about myself from teaching than anything I've taught my students. Before I stepped foot in a classroom, I thought that it would be relatively easy. My thoughts were that all I had to do was master the material I was teaching and be able to manage a bunch of kids. No big deal! What I didn't consider was how my behavior and attitude impacted the atmosphere of my classroom, good and bad.

The intellectual challenge of teaching is not what makes it a difficult job; it's the emotional stress that comes with managing children's behavior. The ability to let things slide without holding a grudge while maintaining a positive attitude took me about three or four years to understand. Before then, to me, most problems I faced were either the students', or administrators', or my colleagues' fault. I was so beaten down with negativity that I wasn't able to see that I was mostly to blame for my misery, not anyone or anything else. Not that children weren't acting bad or that the school could change a few things, because they were, and it could, but the way I responded to my circumstances was judgmental, arrogant, and immature.

My first couple of years, I went to bed and woke up stressed. The first principal I had would hound me, "popping in" my room on an almost daily basis. It was suffocating, and I didn't feel he was giving me freedom to work out my kinks on my own. I was anxious about what he thought of my performance, and I began to dread his presence at work. Being a new teacher, he sensed that I was lost, and his own insecurities led him to feel superior (just my opinion). He would visit my class only to give me gimmicks to implement that he probably picked up in a seminar rather than practical strategies for me to work on. When I set up a meeting to talk to him about how I was feeling overwhelmed and micromanaged, he threw a tantrum as bad as some of my seventh graders! (Ironically, he criticized me and others daily but couldn't take the heat himself.) Somehow, I was able to grind through and keep truckin'. I was blessed with generally well-mannered students that year, but I almost didn't last through the first semester. Needless to say, I wasn't the only person who had issues with him, and as fate would have it, that principal "do no wrong" was fired by year's end, but somehow, I managed to finish the year relatively strong. Over the summer, the district hired a new, much more relatable principal, thank God, but this go-around, the students were the pain in my neck. They were on another level (not in a good way!).

Let me tell you, there's always something to complain about. Until you realize the necessity of finding, digging, and searching for the positive in whatever situation you find yourself, it'll be a long nine months until June. After several years of feeling unhappy with my job and myself, I decided to do something about it. Rather than continue to complain about the same things over and over again, I chose to look inward, and I realized that I had more control over my experience than I gave myself credit for. I can't control other people or certain situations, but I can control my response to them. So I chose to monitor my reactions, emotions, and perspective and what I've come to learn has been life-changing.

To achieve maximum success, you must first hold yourself accountable, even when an issue isn't necessarily your fault. You may not have caused the problem, but you have control over your reaction to it. Each difficult scenario can be resolved or mitigated through self-control, creativity, and actively seeking for solutions. It's much easier to complain and blame others than it is to take responsibility. But the quicker you do, the quicker you'll find what you're looking for.

Know Thyself

A job shouldn't define a person. It's something you do for a living, but it's not who you are. Many people attach most of their identity to their position or job status. Staying well-rounded requires individuals to step outside the monotony of work and find various areas in which to spend their time. It's easy to get caught in a routine of going to work, going home, watch TV, go to sleep—repeat. This happens when there's no passion, goal, or overall sense of importance in one's life outside of their job. You may experience moments of joy when you go out to eat with friends, or grab a drink after a long week, feeling that all the hard work that you put in is worth it for moments like these. The vacations in the summer and all the days off during the year keep some teachers in the grind for years! But without the right attitude, the day-to-day of teaching can seem like a bleak necessity, even with all the extra days off.

Just like children, adults need to have a purpose and direction in their life. The moment we feel that we're not contributing or moving in a positive direction, we'll begin to lessen the value we place on our life and will ultimately settle into lazy and negative patterns like excessive eating, drinking, and entertainment (distraction). If not regulated, these escape mechanisms will zap our energy and life will become a perpetual Groundhog Day: same thing, just a different day. Just like we need a direction, children need guidance so they don't develop bad habits that could take years to untangle. Similar to adults that lack purpose, without proper guidance and direction, they're bound to self-destruct.

When your job is a drag, life can quickly become an obligation where boredom and depression wait with open arms. This shouldn't be the case. We shouldn't drag our feet during the day. Smiles should

31

be real and relationships genuine. But this doesn't happen simply by wanting it, you'll have to do the work!

One's self-concept determines the way in which they see the world and ultimately, how they live their life. A positive self-image is something that each of us needs to work for. Thinking positively is great, but it doesn't become a reality until you put your thoughts into practice. Self-confidence is the first step toward working through any issue you're faced with. It's attainable when you believe that when facing difficult situations, you've got the solution and there's no need to stress out. Whenever we get into a panic, whatever situation comes up, mistakes follow. Self-confidence is a by-product of setting and then working toward accomplishing goals. It's not complicated. Not necessarily easy, but simple in application.

Ask yourself if you see more opportunities or problems in life? Are you taking advantage of what's in front of you? Things like diet, exercise, relationships, work ethic, family, etc. Do you see these things as tools for your development, or are you seeking an escape and a break from responsibility?

Bitterness, complaining, seeing problems instead of opportunities, and choosing what "feels" good over what needs to be done are all signs that you're limiting your potential and, ultimately, fulfillment. I believe that true fulfillment is always on the other end of an obstacle. It's a beautiful dichotomy. Without darkness, how would we know the light? With this in mind, we must accept that discomfort is a part of life. There's no escape from it. So we can either react to life through stress and fear or face it head-on with confidence. When we choose to do things that are uncomfortable yet ultimately good for our health, we can gain control over our stress and productivity.

Most people seek to live their life with as little stress and discomfort as possible. We naturally try to avoid pain at all costs. Back thousands of years ago, people had real worries: lions, bears, invading armies, drought, etc. Now, we live in air-conditioned homes, sit in a car and drive to work, most likely, to sit in a chair once we get there. We're more concerned about likes on social media than we are where our next meal's coming from. No need to hunt down food or tend the farm, there are grocery stores and delivery services to drop food off at our doorstep. In other words, we've got it pretty good. Since we generally have our necessities covered, most of our stress is self-created. If we're living in a constant state of rest, never pushing ourselves at work or in the gym for example, our tendency is often toward laziness, indulgence, and self-centeredness, which all steer us toward a lackluster existence.

In choosing discomfort, we can relieve our bodies and minds of unnecessary stress by generating it ourselves. Exercise is one simple and healthy way to bring discomfort while also relieving stress. It's a free miracle drug, but when we're not in the habit of exercising, it can seem like an unattainable obstacle that we don't want to face. It doesn't have to be exercise, though. Whether it be physical, intellectual, creative, or spiritual, anything that challenges and pushes our minds develops an endurance and confidence that will seep into all areas of our life.

People generally take shortcuts that ultimately lead to self-destruction because of a low self-concept. Those who are confident in themselves believe that they can do whatever they put their mind to, and then they go out and do it. The act of doing is where fulfillment lies. In fact, we're all more capable than we can imagine, but we first must believe it. Those that don't will always look for the easy way out. The fear of failure blinds people from their potential and they'll get stuck, usually in an unfulfilling job, relationship, and life.

The decision to go on a quest and accomplish one's goals is the genesis of development and strength. It's necessary for people to have something to work toward, a purpose and vision, to feel accomplished and fulfilled. When you feel that your life contributes to society and that you provide value to others, self-respect and joy follow. Some teachers have lost or don't see their value. To be effective, you first must believe you can be and that all the hard work involved is worth it. Teachers should possess values like hard work and self-respect in order to be able to pass those qualities on to their students.

Taking shortcuts and just getting by may have some immediate benefits (like not having to face yourself, avoid negative emotions and a quick fix for fear/pain), but down the road it'll lead to chaos. If you don't apply self-control, when things don't work out the way you want them to, the next thing you'll lose is control over your emotions. Without controlling your emotions, they'll have the power to take you over.

The ability to recognize your emotional state without being consumed with the emotion itself is vital for self-control and produces a most important quality: emotional intelligence. If you're not in charge of your emotions, they'll begin to lead and control you which inevitably results in losses throughout your entire life. Whether it's controlling a classroom, or choosing the right meal, self-control will keep you on the path to health and wellness.

Nothing of true value is attained in an instant. In addition to self-control, discipline and commitment are two more essential qualities that lead to a productive life. Consistently making the responsible decision over the convenient one builds routines and habits that will propel you into the next level. Although we don't have control over most events that happen around us, we do have control over how we react to them. Taking responsibility and looking at each situation objectively will help in making appropriate adjustments as we move forward.

Rise Above

Regardless of a student's abilities or attitudes, a calm, collected demeanor will awaken your creativity to solve problems. Effective teachers must develop a warrior's mentality if they want to last an entire school year without beating their head against a wall. Just as in life, teaching is a war. But it's not a war of teachers versus students. The battle isn't external. It's internal—the war is against the self.

If we're being honest and thoroughly turn inward, we'd realize our tendency to allow fear to twist us into behaving just like our "bad students." The root of student's bad behavior is the same for adults, it just manifests differently. What in the world am I insinuating? I'm not saying that you don't pay attention to directions or can't keep your mouth shut when someone else is talking (although that may be true). It's much deeper than that. The difference is that students' problematic behaviors are much easier to point out than adults. Typical bad behavior from students is as follows:

- Talking without permission
- Tardiness
- Failure to do or complete assignments/homework
- Breaking the rules (i.e., chewing gum, cheating, no supplies, etc.)
- Drawing on the desk or in the textbook
- Talking back to teacher
- Bullying, etc.

Now, do teachers exhibit these same behaviors? No, of course not. Or I sure hope not! We're professional working adults, for God's sake! However, many students' behaviors are manifestations of a deeper issue. The difference between a child's behavior and an adult's is that adults have learned to justify and mask their attitudes and biases over the years.

We can become so adapted to our own lazy, procrastinating, and self-justifying behavior that we convince ourselves it's normal and okay. When most people surrounding us—family, friends, coworkers—are stressed out and not living up to their potential, we begin to justify our own lack of productivity or peace of mind. Naturally, we look for and flock to others with similar biases and mind-sets as ourselves, just like kids do. There's just more people and experiences to blame our unproductive, irresponsible, and lazy behavior on. For example, we might blame our parents, an abusive relative, a divorce, or the death of a loved one for our own inadequacies. Paralyzed emotionally with repetitive thoughts of disappointment, we sentence ourselves to mediocrity and, ultimately, frustration. So what do we do? We look for an escape: a drink, cheeseburger, cigarette, or another cup of coffee.

Excuses are learned behaviors that can become ingrained in our thoughts after life hits us so many times. Culture has taught many adults to hide their feelings through learned behaviors. Whether it's overeating, smoking, constantly using social media, gossiping, or any other vices, adults have more of an opportunity to mask their real feelings through external outlets. Adults have cars and money that drive them to avoid their own truth whereas kids are stuck in science lab.

Students don't have the same learned, passive-aggressive masking abilities that many adults have mastered. If they're not feeling good, or have an attitude, they're going to act out. They don't know *not* to show their cards. Their lack of self-control and rational thinking skills are still in process. Teens don't have the luxury of hiding behind the labels that give adults comfort and identity, like a job title or spouse. Nor do they have money to buy entertainment, food, or other stimulation to medicate with. Their mess typically shows up in the classroom.

They're confined to school most days, so naturally their stress is released there. They may start bullying classmates, getting into fights, becoming the class clown, or skipping class in the bathroom, whereas adults run to vices to hide from their reality. These types of behaviors, in both children and adults, are a result of an unwillingness or inability to logically confront and solve problems. The only difference between teachers and students is that teachers have more time (and weight) under their belt.

Life is difficult and full of stressors so learning to manage those moments is essential to keeping a clear head and a positive perspective. Positivity needs to be nourished. The more you use it, the stronger voice it has in your head. As this muscle grows, you'll begin to build a network of positive thoughts that reduce stress and keep your head clear for what's coming. For most, positivity doesn't come naturally. For the pessimists out there (myself included), it's one thing to know you should be positive; it's another to actually be positive.

Positivity is priority number one if you want to be successful. Whether it's exercise, prayer, or meditation, whatever it takes to start the day off on a good note is vital for gaining positive momentum. Consistent, daily reminders to stay positive are necessary, especially when you interact with a colleague who's, let's say, less than pleasant. Or during an obligatory meeting where you're going over test data and seemingly endless reports.

My first few years of teaching was a battle for survival, where I was so worn down and burnt out by the end of the day that my landing spot was typically the couch, with a cold one and a list of television shows to zone out on. Whatever it is that you run to after stressful times to take the edge off can help in the moment, but if you don't take the time to evaluate yourself, you'll miss the gift that's hiding beneath the surface.

Students' off-putting behavior can get your emotions wound up to the point that you lose yourself and start sinking. Instead of looking for an escape on Netflix, the positive response to a wild class is to take some time at the end of the day to look inward and ask yourself a few simple questions:

Did I spend enough time preparing my lesson?
Were students engaged?
Was the lesson understandable?
Did I show enthusiasm?

If the answer was no to one or more of those questions, then you now know what adjustments need to be made to ensure a peaceful ride the next time. Are you willing to do the work? Do you truly desire peaceful days free from unnecessary stress?

If you take responsibility for students' behavior, you'll then be ready for growth. Blaming others for their actions is the easy way out and requires nothing from you. To win in life, you must first take a look at your own actions and learn from others, without judging them.

When you're on your A game, living in your potential and making good decisions for yourself on a daily basis, you'll innately find contentment, confidence, and the ability to love others right where they are. No one should have the power to take you out of your zone. When you're on point, you can have the clarity of mind to not only solve your own personal conflicts but also help others on their journey as well.

Shifting Perspective

Most adults, whether they're conscious of it or not, are stressed for the majority of their lives and don't really know what it feels like without a tinge of anxiety. Stressed out people stress out people. We react to others according to our own emotional state, so if we're constantly stressed or worried, we're going to see people through a lens of fear. This negative filter causes other people to rub us the wrong way especially since we're already headed there. Positive or negative associations with others are created according to our perspective, regardless of their behavior.

One's mindset about the people, places and events of his life will determine his level of joy and effectiveness. For many, what started out as a clean slate and an opportunity for a great year can quickly derail into a struggle to survive if you allow petty nonsense to affect you. (There's a lot of it at schools!) Each difficult person or event that presents itself has the potential to either generate stress or provide with it a lesson to help you grow as an individual.

For example, if your lesson plan isn't engaging students, and they begin to collectively wander off task, you're in store for a long day. They'll disengage and quickly get under your skin. At this point, it's too late to go back and change your lesson entirely. Frustration will linger on your shoulder, tempting you to blame students for their erratic behavior, as if it's their fault they're bored out of their minds! The frustration devil will perch itself on your shoulder and taunt you to start handing out detentions and call parents. (That'll show 'em!) As the swells of stress rise, you'll be eager for a rescue boat to bring you back to shore. Alone in the deep waters of the classroom is where you'll have a decision to make. You can either react in frustration and blame the students for their behavior, or acknowledge your part in the scenario, take responsibility, and respond in wisdom. After a few deep breaths, before you make any phone calls, I think it's wise to consider how you may have contributed to the scenario.

Days in which students behave the worst or aren't engaged are almost always the days when I was least prepared or stressed out myself. It's easy to blame kids for acting up as if it's their fault. And it partially is. However, we're the ones responsible for setting the tone. We have the power to put their fidgeting at ease, but if we're full of anxiety ourselves, what should we expect from them? I can tell you it won't be compliance, order, or a smooth ride to paradise! You'll be lucky if they all behave when you're on your A game much less if you bring a "just good enough," bare minimum attitude.

Moments—yes, moments—that bring the most joy can happen when a handful of positive students enter class in a good mood, work hard, and have good manners. These times are reminders that you are part of building the future, and it's a rewarding feeling. Unfortunately, many of your students can be the opposite. They come to school bringing a lot of chaos with them but are without a pencil. The daily grind in the classroom can seem like an uphill battle, but learning to keep your perspective and calmly manage the stressful moments will put you on the right track to making an impact.

The shift in my perspective from my first year to my fifth was drastic. I initially went into teaching for several reasons. Mainly, because I was getting married, hadn't yet established myself in a "career," and felt that teaching would be a good way to make a solid living while still having enough free time (summer) to pursue other interests. With that being said, I wasn't totally committed to the craft, which left lots of room for mistakes.

I've heard it said that the way someone does one thing is the way they do everything. I tend to agree with that because it's rang true for me in my life. In the classroom, I was giving forth partial effort which led to mediocrity, not only in the classroom, but in every other area of my life: diet, exercise, marriage, friendships, hobbies, etc. I wasn't taking charge of my life and the results showed. I was stressed at work, overweight, struggling in my marriage, lacking meaningful relationships, or the motivation to pursue interests outside of work. I had ideas of how I wanted my life to look, but my lack of confidence limited my belief and proved that I wasn't committed to doing the work that's required to achieve success and happiness. Living defeated by my circumstances and trapped to mediocrity, I didn't realize that all it took was a shift in my perspective to start making simple changes that would impact my entire life.

Teachers obviously aren't in the classroom for the money. There are only so many tax brackets you'll reach grading papers and issuing detentions. For the most part, teachers earn a relatively comfortable salary, depending on who you ask, but it certainly isn't a road to becoming rich and famous. A mostly thankless job without much financial sunshine to look forward to; if you're not careful you can fall into a rut where you're working for the paycheck simply to get by. This can be the beginning of a long, miserable career, sure to bring other problems on the horizon.

Going to work every day feeling that you're underpaid and underappreciated by your students, their parents, and even your administration, can weigh a brother or sister down. But if your perspective remains to be a selfless, strong, positive influence on students needing a healthy, stable adult in their life, you'll have the attitude to accomplish admirable feats. The dollar bills won't be chasing you, but that's not what great teachers are in it for anyway. The most successful ones know they're in a battle.

Maintaining perspective is a precious jewel but can be extremely difficult, especially when you have students rolling their eyes, talking to you as if you're their peer, and cursing like sailors with friends in the hallways. If you find yourself consistently judging and/or cussing their actions under your breath, they'll know. When you feel disdain for someone in your heart, it automatically creates separation.

We all know people that have smiles plastered on their faces. They seemingly wake up happy. Those same people probably never disagree or offer a controversial opinion either. For most, you can bet that smile isn't exactly genuine. If you catch some of those types alone, their resting face probably paints a drastically different picture. This proves the smile isn't conveying joy, but it's a mask of insecurity. You might be able to fake the funk for a while, but over time, the makeup will eventually smear. Children can sniff out a faker from long distances, and if your heart isn't in it, you won't be able to reach them.

Adults often underestimate what children pick up on. They're very perceptive, and they can sense whether you're genuine or not. If you do smile, try to back it up with a listening ear and helpful hand. It's essential to any lasting and healthy bond for consistency. A warm smile from an adult can do wonders for a child overcome with anger or loneliness. However, a smile is only the beginning.

Children are looking for adults who can see them. Someone who looks beyond their exterior and straight to the heart. Attitudes and eye rolls are their toxic way of screaming for help in hopes that you might have a remedy for their frustration. They don't consciously understand that they want your approval and affection. It probably seems like the opposite. Teachers must look past immature behavior, or it'll feel like your students' sole goal is to piss you off and make your day miserable. If all you see is their behavior, you won't be able to help. Underneath the surface of their off-putting behavior lies pain and frustration.

It's extremely important to daily remind yourself that it's your duty as an educator to show up each day with a servant's heart. You're there for them, not the other way around. Irrespective of their behavior, it's the teachers' job to shape students. If they're the ones shaping you, that's a red flag warning you to find your center!

Part of keeping the peace is compassion, especially when you feel like screaming at the top of your lungs! This doesn't mean fake it 'til you make it. That might work for a while, but underneath, if you're not truly compassionate, kids will get the best of you, steal your peace, and make teaching way more difficult than it should be.

Compassion isn't shown by constantly dishing out candy and compliments, either. It doesn't hurt to give rewards but if it's a substitute for your own lack of effort, the sugar high will be short-lived. An overlooked aspect of compassion is discipline. True love always corrects wrongs. It shows you care and will keep the classroom comfortable and safe.

Real impact takes place after a foundation of trust has been established. A trusting relationship with a student is the key to forming connection, which is the key to teaching. Sometimes, getting spit on (metaphorically, but maybe not!), eye rolls, and being on the recipient end of profanity is part of the training. Winning over children with emotional or behavioral problems takes someone who's willing to be repetitively ridiculed without losing confidence in who they are or in what they've been called to do, which is to love. If you can man the storm and keep your peace, you'll at least have a shot at restoring theirs.

Many children experience neglect or are damaged from verbal, physical, emotional, or sexual abuse and, as a result, are paralyzed with fear. Whether that manifests in shyness or anger, they're desperate for someone that's strong enough to accept and care for them regardless of whether they're making straight A's or just being passed on through the system.

Teaching involves much more than challenging the intellect. Good teachers mold the soul. Patience, compassion, and a true love is essential to keeping teachers focused on the objective at hand, which is to inspire and positively influence students. The first quality of love is patience. This is vital. But to stay patient, you must first believe in your ability to handle situations positively.

Discipline

We all have known people who think they're funny but aren't. You know, the annoying guy/gal thirsty for attention? Well, that didn't start when they started working in the cubicle next to you at work. It started on the playground. Some kids can put a grin on your face, but typically, those that do are pleasant and well-behaved most of the time. The one's that put a pain in your neck are those searching for a laugh from their peers—you know, children/teenagers. (Humor is not a requirement to be the star of the show in seventh grade Social Studies!)

Correction or discipline of any kind is a delicate necessity. Unfortunately, the word "no" can be a foreign concept to many kids these days, and if it is, they'll probably take it like a personal attack. When there's no one in their life setting boundaries and limitations, when teachers do, students don't understand how to process it. This puts teachers on the brunt end of their attitudes. If you lose your cool, get smart with them, or fail to correct their behavior calmly, they'll likely dig their little heels in even more, out of spite.

Sorry, but you can't paddle children for being punks anymore. There are laws against that now. Sort of kidding. But seriously, the ol' fallback "Back when I was in school…" needs to go back to where you aren't. Stop it! You're not in school (as a student), you're the teacher now, so to put it bluntly: either get with the program and adjust to reality or find another way to pay the bills!

When schools were encouraged to use physical punishment, I'm sure classroom behavior was a lot more subservient (and people were more inclined to behave in general), but we're in a much different era now. Not only have the laws changed, but society and culture has as well.

Sensitivity is, well, highly sensitive these days. Schools cater to the emotional needs of students to a much higher degree, making it necessary for teachers to make the appropriate adjustments. Brute force and "because I said so" doesn't carry the same weight as it used to. In the past, most children did what they were told by adults… because… they were told to! There wasn't much wiggle room for debate. If authority was questioned, you got smacked! Not so anymore, my friend, not so…

It is a good thing that we've moved on from enforcing violence toward taking a more thoughtful approach. It's also productive for children (and adults) to ask thoughtful questions about why things are the way they are. When questions aren't answered, confusion and anger can be justified. Teachers should be able to answer questions regarding certain rules and expectations. Children usually don't understand why order and discipline is necessary for everyone's safety, until someone explains it to them.

Taking time to explain shows that you care. If you're stuck in an old school mind-set, unwilling to walk students through seemingly obvious questions, you could be considered the worst thing to be thought of in these sensitive times—a bully! If you're unwilling or unable to expound on why things are the way things are, then who's the ignorant one?

Students need to know that you're confident and that nonsense won't be tolerated. It's one thing to say the right words, but if your actions don't line up, then it's only a matter of time for these little lions to roar. As society continues to lean in a more sensitive direction, the only way to keep your head above water is first, accept this reality, and second, adjust and get creative in the way you communicate to students.

Should teachers correct misbehavior? Of course. Don't ever let kids get away with chaos. Correction isn't the issue. It's how you do it and your emotional response to their behavior. Keeping your center, or not, as storms blow through will reveal who's really in charge—you or your students.

Some teachers are laid back while others are rigid and demanding. Everyone has their own way of doing things and that's okay. We all have our moments, and there will be times when making threats and demands seems appealing. This, however, can cause teachers to age quicker than middle schoolers.

As teachers, we have expectations for our students and get easily frustrated when children behave like children! An instinctual reaction to unruly behavior or disrespectful attitudes can be either shock or old-fashioned anger. You mean a child just said that? To their teacher? Be prepared to handle all the issues that come with students' confusion, anger, fear, and boredom.

Disrespect toward teachers is an inevitable hurdle you'll have to leap, and some students have a seeming complete disregard for rules and authority. They talk to their teachers as if they're the boss; where the bold ones have no fear of consequences, the beautiful think they're always right, and as the year turns, calling parents and suspensions often do little in changing their dramatic soap opera behavior. In fact, some even want to get suspended. They see it as a vacation where they can get a break from sitting in a classroom. The reality is, they may just be biding their time until they're old enough to legally drop out.

Children carrying this mentality will most likely seek the admiration of their classmates, rather than teachers, vying to be the center of attention. Through either tardiness, joking, or excessive talking, their sole goal may just be to piss off the teacher and go back to ISS (In School Suspension) or sit in the counselor's office. They'll require constant restraint and objectivity on your part. How do you get through to children who are thirsting for attention and hell-bent on getting it from their peers?

STAY CALM

Every child possesses unique gifts, personalities, and abilities. Teachers should seek to water their seeds of talent, and it should be a passion to mold and steer students toward success. Realizing their potential and naive innocence should motivate us as we lead them to the light, in whatever subject or life skill we're trying to instill. However, there are some students who seemingly object to success. No matter how patient or caring you may be, they may seem determined to get off track. In circumstances like these, if you're unable to reach them, then you need to at least make sure they don't cause you unnecessary stress. Staying calm, collected, without taking their behavior personally is the beginning of managing toxic situations.

You know where your heart lies when you have students like these. Nothing other than patient, gentle guidance will get these children back on track. If you react with anger, one of two things will happen. One, they'll come right back at you with more of their attitude. Or two, they'll likely withdraw and shy away.

Yelling at children for misbehaving should be considered a last resort. If an entire class is acting up, then yelling might be the only thing that gets their attention in the moment, but this should very rarely be the case. When anger rises to the surface, some teachers make it a point to let students know: "They'd better not do it again, or else!" If the students continue to act up, the teacher will yell twice as loud and maybe even start handing out detentions.

Whether in the moment or after the fact, teachers are probably thinking something like *How dare that disrespectful brat misbehave in my classroom!* Most times, yelling at children will lose its effect, especially if it's something that's done on a regular basis. After a while, the yelling becomes obsolete, students will stop listening and bad behavior continues, if not get worse. When students know they can get under your skin and throw you off center, they'll lose their respect. You can gain it back, but it'll take that much more of their off-putting behavior before you do.

Yelling is usually the result of a lack of creativity and resolve. Children can sniff out insecure, insincere, nervous, unprepared, or fearful teachers. They're very instinctual, and if they know you're off your game, it'll be a long, uphill battle moving forward. Unpreparedness, disorganization, or habitual negativity are some characteristics that qualify teachers to get walked over by their students.

Attitudes may pop off after enforcing discipline or after making corrections on an assignment, and if the teacher doesn't handle these situations wisely, instead of acting out, many students will pull back from you. A little of your own attitude or visible frustration is all it takes for you to push them away. These incidents can nullify any potential hard work from them moving forward, and once they feel uncomfortable or lose respect for you, it can be difficult to reel them back in. As a teacher, it's a priority to keep your calm and maintain perspective when dealing with unruly/unacceptable behavior.

For example, students will have their phones out when they shouldn't. They'll text, get on social media, whatever. When this happens, one thing to remember is that you can't deal with every student the same way. Before speaking, calm yourself. Keep your emotions in check and choose your words carefully. The energy you emanate will determine their response. If you stay cool, the more likely they will too. Gently reminding the student that cell phones aren't permitted, without an angry expression or tone of voice is ideal. Any frustration in your voice will build upon negativity.

Children for whom this book is not written will do what you say, no problems. The disobedient/rebellious ones are our focus here, and they are almost always the most sensitive to correction. Believe it or not, they're not a lost cause, but it's easy to think that way. The default mentality for those tasked to instruct the rebels is that they're just a problem, nothing but trouble. Obviously, this mind-set won't win you any victories.

There's always hope, even if it's nearly impossible to see. Your job is to look past their deviance or laziness, be the authority, and impact their behavior through positive encouragement. This isn't our natural inclination and can be a daily battle, but it's necessary for your own peace of mind. Any excuses that justify your own negativity can't be an option or you'll slip back into the daily, monotonous grind without much to look forward to.

Rules or Relationship?

The stressed out, screaming loud, too proud to love a child attitude will wear you out. Who wants that? Intimidation may help keep students in line for a moment, but in the long run you'll lose your chance at making a connection or a lasting impact. Hopefully teachers are educators for the challenge of making a difference in the lives of kids. Unfortunately, many teachers don't believe that forming bonds with their students is important, and they spend the entirety of their careers thinking the best way to manage a classroom is by scaring students into submission. Believe that if you may, but my experience has shown me that it's much less stressful staying cool and calm. Patience shown toward students, whether it's their behavior or academic performance, can make or break the relationship and will be a tremendous help as you lead the way.

Another reason a teacher may want to rule their class with an iron fist is the fear of the unknown. This happens when you're so concerned with students getting out of hand that you overcompensate by enforcing a lot of rigid rules. With this outlook, one's peace of mind is dependent on his ability to control students' behavior. For example, after several students talk out of turn or blurt something out in the middle of instruction for the umpteenth time, teachers might instinctually get fed up with it, lose their patience, and yell, possibly throwing in some threats and demands. After a while, this strategy will create more problems and never gets to the root of the issue.

Teachers who use fear and intimidation usually are doing that out of their own fear—mainly the fear of losing control. Optimally, teachers should gain the respect of their students without striking fear. Students need to know that their teachers care about them as individuals, not just that they want them to make a good grade on their exams. If they feel that you care about them as people, you can make a greater impact on their world and they just may give you some gratification as well.

Teachers also act tough because they want to hide behind their rough exterior. Intimidation is a tactic used by those who may have difficulty making connections with people, and it creates distance, which makes teaching much more difficult. Teachers can be private people and may not want to get personal with their students, but in order to make an impact, a bond of some sort is necessary for optimal performance for both the student and teacher. Students who are comfortable and at peace with their teachers will perform better in the classroom. If they're intimidated, they may follow rules, but anxiety can limit their academic focus.

Some believe that vulnerability will cause them to lose their students' respect, but in reality, the opposite is true. If you have the confidence to show vulnerability, then they'll trust you. Respect follows relationship, not the other way around. Intimidation incites fear and negates trust. There needs to be a level of trust between both parties for a real connection to be made. The unspoken qualities of one's character trumps rules and threats. With thick skin, the right perspective, and a compassionate heart, you'll have the best chance at winning over theirs.

Commanding respect is something that many teachers don't understand. As the leader of the classroom, teachers should command the respect of their students, but not in the ways one might expect. It doesn't come from a list of rules, threats, detentions, or rigorous work. Those things can be effective, but if you really want to take command, in your classroom or your life for that matter, you first must learn to command yourself. This will keep you from making a laundry list of threats, rules, and consequences to keep children in check. When a teacher's in control of himself, students naturally fall in line.

People respond to energy, especially children. A self-assured, prepared, and positive adult can take control of a classroom without even saying a word. Respect primarily comes from unspoken actions, attitudes, and the ways in which one carries himself. Power lies behind a confident spirit and when people believe in themselves, others take note. Authority doesn't mean that you demand obedience to a ton of strict rules and expectations. Yes, you need to set expectations, but the heart of the issue lies in how you enforce your authority.

Discipline Protocol

There are necessary courses of action for teachers correcting students' behavior, one being reaching out to parents. However, at times, this can seem like searching for a fugitive, or walking into a lion's den. Either you can't find them due to a wrong number in the directory, or when you do make contact, they get defensive and won't concede to the fact that their little angel might not be one of light, if you know what I mean!

Instead of looking at the situation objectively, parents often become defensive and make excuses, putting the blame on others (teachers do this as well!). Most likely, in their minds, the reason their child's acting inappropriately in your classroom is because of you! They'll heed a story from their child rather than the teacher to avoid taking any responsibility.

Many parents would rather make excuses, so they don't have to admit their own weaknesses or faults. If parents would humble themselves and open their minds up enough to receive feedback, they could then work with teachers for the betterment of the child. An objective opinion from a teacher can give parents a healthy perspective of situations they're not aware of. For most parents, it's tough to see the forest through all the trees.

If reaching out to parents doesn't help, the next step would be to follow up with administration or a school counselor. Each school/district has policies that are mandated for appropriate discipline to be enforced. You can't make them do push-ups or run laps, and the paddles have been retired. So unless it's a situation of violence or drug use, beyond talking to parents and counselors, there's only so much discipline that administration can implement.

I don't know about your thoughts on detention, but in my case, staying after school rather than getting on with my evening is just as much a punishment for me as it is the student. I don't want to stay late at work just to prove a point to an unruly child! I'd rather be able to handle the situation in the moment without having to resort to that. All detention does is create more work for the teacher while angering an already unstable child. So rather than yelling and handing out punishments, maybe the scary disciplinarian teacher can take a different angle. If whatever measures haven't worked so far, then your own creativity is the necessary final step. Since you're limited in what you can do regarding discipline, creativity is a must.

An important note to remember in all this is that initially, a positive, genuine relationship with your students should negate most potential flare-ups in the classroom. When an authentic bond is formed, you'll have their trust and the authority to motivate them to excel. The biggest key to changing students' behavior is to sincerely seek a relationship with them, especially the ones that continuously act up. Try talking to them as individuals. Let them know you're not the enemy and that you want the best for them.

PARENTS

Every school year, parents will ask, "What can I do to help my child succeed?" And every year, the answer probably sounds something to the tune of "If they start struggling, make sure they attend tutoring" or maybe "Ask your child what their homework is every day after school and check to see if they complete it. If you sense your child's not performing well, stay in contact with their teachers. Schedule a conference if you feel it's necessary." You might even suggest they encourage their child to sit down and read every evening for at least twenty to thirty minutes. (Common sense!) Although those are generic responses, they're still good suggestions. Unfortunately, they don't address the unique, unpredictable, and fluid reality of a child's development, not to mention the mind-set of an inexperienced or overwhelmed parent.

Parenting is the most important job an individual can endeavor to take on. It requires responsibility, time, attentiveness, money, and, most importantly, love. Ideally, as we develop personally over time, we'll attain wisdom and understanding about ourselves and the world. The next natural step would be to have children and hopefully instill in them the values we've gained over our life experience to that point in hopes that they'll go on to do better than ourselves, but unfortunately, this is rarely the reality in today's world.

When adults are willing to objectively take personal responsibility for themselves and their family, then everyone, especially the children, benefit. Unfortunately, many parents, for various reasons, are unwilling or unable to parent their children in ways they deserve. A major challenge for teachers is to accept this dim reality and choose to find ways to overcome the obstacles they'll face rather than complain and make excuses about them.

A major crisis in society is children raising children. Just because one reaches a certain age doesn't mean he's an adult. Legally, yes, but in terms of having developed as a person capable of passing down wisdom, the sad truth is that many "adults" have little to offer. Emotionally stunted, many get stuck with the mind-set and emotional intelligence of a child. How do I know this? For example, stop and take note of someone with temper issues. They pop off easily and consistently, lacking self-control, like a child. Or those that blame their problems in their life on others and rarely take responsibility. They find every little thing to complain about. Vices like alcohol, junk food, social media, or television dominate their time and suffocate productivity.

Vices can become quick fixes for those that are stressed and lacking purpose in life. They're shortcuts to "feeling better," which is always the result of a lack of discipline and self-control, two essential qualities of a healthy, functioning adult. If we want the world to run smoother, now and in the future, adults need to ask themselves if they're laying the groundwork for that to happen. Children need someone to model responsibility if they're going to grow to be successful themselves.

Beyond basic curriculum, learning to manage time and emotions is often an overlooked quality in schools. Emotional intelligence is vital for success in all areas of life, but if you hope to pass it on to the coming generation, you must have it yourself. The lack of emotionally healthy parents and teachers has resulted in lost, frustrated and scared children yearning for a real man or woman to show them the way. Children aren't "evil" because they're born that way. It's natural for them to act up, but it's just as necessary for someone to be there to firmly and lovingly correct their behavior. Without instilling proper discipline, parents can unknowingly create little monsters who lack the capacity to grow into productive adults capable of improving upon society.

When children have little to no guidance and/or discipline, they feel free to act out on their fantasies. Drugs, alcohol, sex, gossip and fighting are common behaviors when there's a lack of discipline or love in their life. As children delve into these areas, you can be sure it's a result of pent up and suppressed emotions, most likely stemming from the home.

Many children are living in constant anxiety because they don't trust their parents (or adults in general). This may simply be due to a busy mom or dad who's not taking the time to emotionally connect with them. Some parents may work long hours trying to keep up with bills and put food on the table and don't have the time or capability to give their children the guidance they need. By the time they get home from work, they're either too exhausted to connect with their children, or it's so late that everyone is already in bed.

Children react, respond to, and are shaped by their atmosphere. If raised with love, attention, joy and discipline, kids will inevitably grow to be contributors in the world. If they're not getting emotional nourishment the cycle of fear, anger, and frustration will repeat and the kids we're raising today will raise more just like them.

Regardless of the situation, distracted parents may not realize the importance of their presence in a child's life. It's vital for teachers to realize what their students may be dealing with so that they can be ready to fill in the gaps where they can.

People look for comfort through consistency. When it's lacking at home, kids will look for it elsewhere and if that's the case, it probably won't be conducive to productivity. Schools are often the one place of consistency in children's lives when they have parents who lack the time necessary to healthily invest in their lives. Simple actions like checking on grades, monitoring friendships and even keeping an eye on their social media activity takes energy that many parents are either unwilling or unable to provide.

Some children are responsible for getting themselves out of bed and out the door to catch the bus. There isn't a hot breakfast on the table or a good morning greeting/hug. Clothes aren't ironed, teeth may not get brushed. These simple yet necessary actions are often neglected, and the kid suffers.

Do these busy parents love their kids? Most likely the answer is a resounding *yes*, of course, they do! That's why they're working those long hours. But more often than not, these long hours on the job are taking them away from the time necessary to develop the bonds that children need and crave. A few less dollars in the bank probably wouldn't kill some parents. Those dollars they're working so hard for may just end up in the hands of therapists and psychiatrists down the road anyway! After basic financial needs are met, parents should focus primarily on raising healthy, responsible and respectful children. Unfortunately, these days it can be tough to find adults who meet that criteria! How can unhealthy, irresponsible and disrespectful adults be capable of raising a healthy and productive child? The answer is simple. They can't.

Intentional or not, good or bad, initial craft/art/and cultivation of life starts at home. When parents fail to enforce discipline, teachers often become the ones in charge of confronting, teaching, and explaining to children that certain behaviors and choices always have consequences. School should be an additional tool, not the foundation of a child's education or it becomes a playground for them to release pent up, negative emotions. Without guidance at home, students will inevitably act out in school. Why? Because they don't know any better.

Children are sponges who take on the atmosphere surrounding them. If they're among chaos at home and have never been taught fundamental values, it's only a matter of time until they manifest that environment at school. Undisciplined children don't understand consequences at school because they're probably not getting them at home. These students typically react with anger and confusion to the dreaded word "no." Shocking!

Parents will get mad when their kid acts up, neglecting the fact that leading up to their child's deviance they, mom and/or dad, had little interest at all in the details of their child's life. They're shocked when their kid does something out of line, as if they had no idea their kid was capable of such things. Clueless to the reality that if left unmonitored and unmolded, kids (and adults) are inclined to chaos. In this case, the parents should be the ones who get a lecture before their kid does.

Believe it or not, teachers do not get pleasure out of spending their personal time after school calling parents because a student can't seem to behave appropriately. (If a teacher does have some sick pleasure in punishing children then you can bet their classroom, and life, is a dark cave of negativity!) Correction is an important aspect of care and any good teacher will take the time to alert parents if their child is continuously acting up. However, teachers would much rather be grading papers, planning lessons, or honestly, headed home to their own lives once the final bell rings. After a full day of rounding up children, the last thing teachers want to do is deliver the unfortunate news to a parent that their kid is either struggling academically or plain acting a fool.

Children need, even desire, structure, boundaries, and limits; not just at school, but especially at home! Discipline provides a sense of peace and control for kids, and it shows that someone cares and believes in them. Just like at school, they may not understand or may hate rules, but whether they know it or not, rules protect them and provide a safeguard against potential hazards. After teachers have exhausted all their tools, they've talked to the student, called home, and notified administration, if the child's bad behavior continues, eventually it falls back on parents to instill some common sense, or the student's deviance will inevitably take them to the fast lane of failure. Unfortunately, the discipline that some of these kids need goes beyond the limitations of what a teacher can provide. If we want children to have confidence and success and to learn what their interests are, it will require parents to invest time in their children, beyond what schools are capable of.

Two Eyes, Two Ears, One Mouth

Good parenting requires a sacrifice of *time*. Children are the future and we need to guide them there. Left to their own devices, well, if you've read *Lord of the Flies*, the kids kill each other! Children don't have the right to tell parents (authority) what's okay for them. That's why they need parents!

Stop the trouble before it starts. It takes time and effort. Commit to being there for your kids. Invest in their emotions. Encourage and tell them they can be successful, but more importantly, lead by your actions. It starts with you! If you can't, aren't willing to, or don't know how to love, don't blame the child, it's not their fault! They're reacting to the environment that's created at home.

If you're not present or aware of their feelings, they'll take direction in life from something or someone else. Whether it's meeting basic needs like food and shelter or taking them to soccer practice, children need adults that take time to show them their value. Unlike adults, young children don't care about money. They just want someone to give them attention. We only start caring about the superficial stuff like shoes and being popular when our ego wakes up, usually around middle school. As we become more aware of the world around us, society convinces us that we're not good enough being who we already are. Children want love and so do adults. But the genius of kids is that they know it's found in relationship, not money or things.

The opposite of love is fear. Fear is the true "F" and is the root cause of every problem in life. In extreme cases, some children don't know where their next meal will come from. They may have been abandoned or abused by their family. On the other end of the spectrum, they might just be lacking words of encouragement, positive reinforcement, or necessary discipline when they get off track. The result in children from of all these scenarios is still fear. Most issues a child faces in life can be overcome when parents are willing to take the time to show authentic love. It's an anchor that can withstand the storms all children face at school and will keep their head above water when the swells seem to be crashing over their heads.

When a child is gripped by fear, they'll develop emotional coping mechanisms and will seek comfort through various means. Whether it's food, drugs, premature romance, or acting up merely for attention, fear is the catapult for all kinds of dysfunction, including a low self-esteem. Whether its bullying, falling in with the bad crowd, or slacking off on homework, a strong self-esteem, resulting from loving support at home, can carry them through each storm.

How do you develop a child's self-esteem? Spend quality time with them. Listen to them. Honor their thoughts and feelings. Allow them freedom to express themselves without them fearing judgment or condemnation. When parents aren't involved in their child's life and don't notice certain unruly behaviors, they'll fall through the cracks and act out in one way or another. This is their way of crying for help.

Pursuing authentic relationships with children generally keeps their emotions above water. Deep levels of communication will provide them with the support they'll need to prevent an unwanted episode at home or at school. When a child doesn't get support or feels isolated, they'll either internalize their emotions or act out. The former leads to depression, the latter gets them in trouble. If parents could see what they're doing (or not doing) that's causing their child pain, they could fix the root of the problem, which is oftentimes themselves. Instead, most parents hire a therapist and see if they can "fix the problem." Nothing wrong with therapy, if the right person is getting it for the right reasons.

When parents are involved and interested in their children, most deviance is annulled. Involvement doesn't mean just spending time. It's the quality of time that's most important. Parents often project their children into the image that they want them to be, unable to see the unique individual that's inside. They're more focused on superficial labels that society creates so that they can judge and assess their child's seeming value. Things like grades, athletic ability, talent, good looks, and popularity are some of the primary qualities that get the most love and attention from parents, teachers, and other students.

In the world today, thoughts and emotions are secondary to accomplishment and "success." We've got to move past predefined labels and toward the heart. When parents get interested in connecting with their kid on a level beyond materialism and superficiality, they'll both find true relationship and joy.

Family Dynamics

Family values are deteriorating in our society. Divorce rates are through the roof, forcing many children to grow up in broken families. Single parent homes often create fear within children that can lead to behavioral issues down the line. Children feel most secure within the loving confines of both their biological parents. The miraculous bond between child and parent is the most natural relationship a human being can experience. We are our parents' DNA and a piece of them whether we like it or not.

Without the full compass of a mother and father's love, children often succumb to feelings of inadequacy because they're lacking either the nurturing care of a mother or more likely, the masculine security of a father. Without going into a tirade on proper roles within a family, there are some obvious strengths that men and women have that differ from one another. Mainly, that men are physically stronger and less emotional, usually. When a father isn't present, oftentimes children may not receive the level of discipline that's needed. On the other hand, women are often gentler and have a more nurturing nature. If a mother's absent, children lack the comfort that mothers can provide. So what happens when one parent is absent? The other will try to overcompensate for the absence of their partner. Nature designed us with strengths and weaknesses. Trying to fit in a box we weren't created for causes unnecessary stress within the parents and affects the entire family dynamic.

Not to say that a single parent can't raise a child to become an accomplished, healthy adult; there are plenty of wonderful single parents out there doing an amazing job! However, in an ideal world, if all parents could raise children with a loving, responsible, and healthy partner, there would be a much-greater chance of their child reaching his potential. Oftentimes though, depending on the circumstance, that may not be possible. The point is that there's a greater chance of a negative or toxic family dynamic when the support of both (hopefully healthy) parents is lacking.

When arguments, frustration, addictions, and stress prevail, the children suffer. Whether there are two parents or one in a home, the first priority of parents should be to maintain a loving and peaceful atmosphere. Children haven't developed the wisdom or strength necessary for handling toxic situations. No matter how great a mother or father is, children always feel the most loved when both parents are involved. Unless a child's born with an iron will or a natural optimism, when parents are absent, emotional problems lie waiting on the horizon.

Basic qualities such as self-esteem, responsibility, manners, and respect all begin at home, not school. Outside influences like teachers, coaches, and even friends can have some effect, but a child's home is the loudest and most influential voice they'll hear. Some provide an atmosphere of love and support. Others are chaotic, stressful, and even dangerous, where fear dominates the room and inevitably creates unnecessary stresses on a child, severely limiting their growth in all areas. Home should be a place of refuge, refueling, and refinement; when it's not, negative outcomes await.

Any system or structure, that is, business or family, that's compromised will force the other parts to abandon their primary role so that they can tend to the weaknesses caused by the missing part. This is true in sports, business, and families. Having both parents in the home is foundational, but when they are around, they need to be emotionally healthy themselves, or they, too, can create an even more toxic environment than a healthy single parent's home will.

If a child is raised by healthy and loving parents, excelling in school is usually a natural by-product. This doesn't mean that all kids with a happy home will always make straight A's, but involved parents will do everything they can to provide their kid with the help they may need. The opposite is also true. Show me one bully, flunk out, or student with behavioral issues that's not coupled with problems at home. I propose that most, if not all, children who are constantly having their parents called due to low grades or bad behavior are simply manifesting the dysfunction they're feeling from home.

When schools solely focus on student's behavior, we'll continue to stay stuck, and stressed. Their behavior is only what we see on the surface. Society should be focused on the root of the issue, the adults in charge of their care. Should children get away with cussing out a classmate, cheating on a test, or vandalizing school property? No, they should get punished. But most likely when they're caught dipping their toes in muddy waters, it wasn't the first time that they've veered off, just the first time they got caught.

It's the duty of parents to safeguard their children, most importantly by building a trusting relationship. When parents don't take the time to know and understand their child's emotions, dreams, desires, fears, and interests, they'll find those connections they crave somewhere else. So don't blame them when they do, say, or believe something crazy. Parents have the authority to make a lasting impact.

Cell Phones

Children living in a world without limitation and lacking sufficient discipline can make teaching in the public school system comparable to herding cats. The society we live in today neglects what's truly important. It has slowly devalued love and family and instead promotes materialism and the image of success.

Do we need to make money? Of course. But that doesn't mean you have to "keep up with the Joneses." Many parents are overworked and overstressed to the point that by the time they get home to their families, there's little left in the tank for their family. Most are more concerned with either their next promotion or drink than they are, say, their children's grades or choice of friends. After work, stressed out parents seek to detach and decompress and get sucked into chasing distractions.

When parents are disengaged from themselves and their family, cell phones and media become the most influential voice in not only their life but their child's as well. Some may think that if Johnny or Suzy is quiet in their room, all's good. Television, video games, and social media give the illusion that things are calm and okay, when inside our heads and our families, chaos abounds. If parents don't actively seek relationship with their children, they're unknowingly opening doors to potential destructive patterns that can take years to reverse.

Cell phones provide us with access to communication and information like never before. People are more glued to their phones than the *life* that's happening around them. It's easy to be tricked into the mind break that cell phones / social media pull us into. Whenever there's a pause in action, like a line at the grocery store, for example, you can bet you'll see someone staring at their screen. We don't have the same ability to wait and reside in the moment like we used to because of all the distractions beckoning for our attention.

Cell phones are like pizza for the mind. They're fun, but if you eat pizza for every meal, excess weight starts piling up. We need structures, limits, and guidance which most don't implement in their own life, much less their child's. Instead, many people are constantly zoned out on their phones, and for some, it seemingly never stops. Whether it's an update, selfie, post, or tweet, most are chasing an escape at every free moment, and our children are following suit. When used appropriately smart phones are wonderful tools, but like anything, if abused or misused, they can become a major source of distraction.

I rarely see children going outside or playing with toys anymore. How long ago was it when they didn't have iPads, phones, or gaming systems to zone them out? How did they behave? How did you behave? What did parents do with anxious and fidgety children twenty to thirty years ago? Now we have screens (and medications)—convenient sedatives for busy parents. We're living in the digital age where social media captivates minds and, if not monitored, can lead to dangerous playgrounds. Back in the good ol' days when kids ran around outside for fun, the last thing a parent would allow is for their child to go barefoot. When going to the park, responsibility warns parents of potential dangers like broken glass or dog poop, scattered among the gravel. Common sense tells parents to make sure kids are wearing shoes, so they don't cut their foot on glass or step in a stinky mess. In the same way, parents should also make sure to administer boundaries for the playground of the web.

Phones give kids access to all sorts of perversities. On the internet, there aren't lifeguards, police officers, or babysitters to keep an eye on what they might look up. Sure, you can set up parental restrictions, but those don't block every little dirty thing out there. For example, if kids get ahold of unflattering or sensitive pictures of their classmates, it can spread like wildfire and do drastic damage to a child's reputation and confidence. Things like "sexting" happen between children in middle school, if not elementary! Not only are kids being exposed to adult content, but they're exposing their bodies to each other. Times are changing, and so should our awareness of them.

If parents think that their child needs a phone, set up some guidelines and timeframes. iPads, phones, and screens in general shouldn't be accessible to a child all day and night. Sure, they're welcome distractions for parents trying to corral hyper, bored, or annoying kids but that doesn't mean parents should stop parenting.

Unfortunately, the internet, and technology in general, has become a crutch that many parents rely on when they're too stressed or distracted to give children the attention they crave, and it's starting while their kid is still in diapers. Not to say that watching movies and playing games is totally wrong! That's not the point. I think they're great attention-grabbers that can help parents survive the trenches. But like anything, there needs to be a balance. Unrestricted cell phone use and social media, degrading music, junk food, and various other negative influences are brainwashing the minds of youth. Some kids never have a moment without their phone. They're addicted and might have a full panic attack if they're without it for ten minutes!

Let the kid play on the phone or watch a show or two, but make sure to talk and relate to them as well. Communicate that you're interested in what's going on in their world. Kids who're constantly distracted by games, the internet, television, etc. without consistent attention from their parents can start to believe, consciously or not, that they're not important. They'll look to celebrities, Twitter, friends, food, drugs, whatever to fill their need for the connections that are meant for parents and loved ones to satisfy. The next thing you know, the kid's having trouble at school, hanging out with the wrong crowd, and parents have no idea why! Without consistent times of bonding, guidance, and discipline, children will turn to friends at school for the attention they're not getting at home.

This ain't 1958, or even '98. We're well beyond 2000, and the world is moving at a speed in which we've never seen! So we'd better keep up and evolve with the times or things will get even more out of control. There's a level of focus necessary for parents to stay active in their kid's life, and if not, something or someone else will gain their affection. Don't let the flies lord over their lives!

Nutrition

Our diet is foundational for not only our physical bodies but also our mental performance. Without proper nutrition and exercise, it's only a matter of time before disease rears its head. Society is every day becoming more of a fast-paced race for instant gratification where health is often the first thing that gets overlooked, and it's trickling down to our children. As we enter the adult world, many are seduced into the hamster wheel of chasing more money, or "likes" on Instagram. In this pursuit, stress piles up and self-control wanes. In the rat race of life, media convinces us we need more "stuff," while the little devil perched on our shoulders tempts us to run toward greasy dinners and stiff drinks to ease the pain of the daily grind.

When adults are too stressed to properly care for themselves, children get the leftovers of our stressed and lackadaisical approach to health. What we eat has a huge impact on our mood, energy, and concentration. If we're not taking care of ourselves, it's foolish to think that children will. Many kids are left unmonitored with their friends and social media, but also their *diet*. Some children are eating candy, salty chips, and drinking soda on a more than regular basis, at school and at home. Many students rarely eat a balanced meal, and we wonder why they have behavioral problems! How in the world is a child on a constant sugar high supposed to sit still and concentrate for a class, much less an entire school day? And when they crash, game over!

Processed food is not only terrible for the body, but it bogs you down mentally. The food that's provided in school cafeterias isn't exactly known for its nutritional value. It's cheap, easy to produce, and usually sees a trash can before it does a belly—unless of course it's pizza day! There's nothing wrong with a good pizza or a juicy burger every now and then, but if you're constantly eating junk, your body eventually will fall apart. Mixing in foods like fruits and vegetables isn't fun, but the positive results far outweigh the momentary gratification that junk food provides.

Parents who take the time to prepare meals for their children understand the value of a healthy diet. Now, stop and take a moment to reflect. Think about children and their behavior, then look at… yourself. Would you want your children or students following in your footsteps? Are you living your best life? If not, don't blame the children for their dysfunctional behavior, they're just reacting to what's around them.

The System

In no other scenario do children gather as consistently and for such a length of time than at school. Some benefits schools provide are that they give kids an opportunity to learn new subject areas while developing interpersonal skills in hopes of discovering their niche.

Hundreds of years ago, children learned directly from a master of their craft. They were apprenticed to learn a trade from an early age. Back in the day, if Papa was a shoemaker, then son was making shoes, whether he liked it or not. Before the technological boom of the printing press and, much more recently, the internet, people's options were much more limited. Now we have schools that expose children to various subjects in hopes that by the time they graduate, they've figured out a path that works best for them.

While they're learning math equations and sentence structure, they're also exploring who they are and which direction they want to take in life. Exposing children to different subjects like science and language arts is an important aspect in developing a well-rounded curriculum, and hopefully, with the help of some elective classes like art, music, or athletics, students can discover their unique gifts and talents.

However, due to its systemized platform, public school limits freedom of expression and creative thinking, often shutting out otherwise very intelligent and out-of-the-box thinkers. A major setback is that students are clumped together regardless of ability, learning the same facts from the same core curriculum. One of the most difficult aspects of teaching in a public school is that you'll have students with abilities across the board, from A-honor roll superstars down to kids who never should've passed their previous two to three grade levels. Keeping the highly intelligent engaged while making sure you don't lose the lower level students is a challenge that teachers constantly face.

In an ideal situation, children could be grouped from an early age with others sharing their same aptitudes, interest and gifts. This would enable them to glean from each other while sharpening their natural talents. It would also allow them to discover and focus on their passions and eventually become experts in their desired field. When we're focused on sharpening our talents, we build the confidence necessary to excel. If students had a way of discovering what their gifts were from an early age, they'd be quicker and more confident in pursuing their desired industry or career. Since students are forced into learning the exact same facts, it can limit opportunities for them to explore and express their unique perspective. If a student is a visionary, daydreamer, or deep thinker, they can be misunderstood by their teachers, which can cause much unnecessary conflict and may potentially damage their confidence. It's important to approach each child with the understanding that they're unique and may not fit in the system with most other children. Some will require just a little more patience and attention. The public school system isn't designed to pinpoint a child's unique abilities, it's more concerned about preparing kids for state-mandated tests!

Beyond assignments and activities, school mainly consists of following directions, obeying teacher's orders, completing assignments, and a lot of fact memorization. For many students, grades 1–12 is a monotonous experience that they're forced into, but it's the reality of the day. Working their way through the system, students grind through high school and are encouraged to go for another four years at a university which can be a daunting reality.

There are pros and cons to a college degree, but these days, a bachelor's degree is more akin to what a high school diploma used to be—it just doesn't carry the same weight as it did, say thirty or so years ago. More and more college graduates are buried in student loans or end up serving Frappuccinos while living with their parents. In the competitive world we live in today, having a college degree is only the beginning. If children aren't taught the value of hard work and discipline, they'll get lost among the masses who are all shooting for similar goals. As the world continues to evolve, we need to broaden our horizons of what education and intelligence looks like. School is foundational, good grades are necessary, but we could all benefit from looking beyond academics into what it takes to be successful.

CONCLUSION

As adults, it's our responsibility to take it upon ourselves to be the best person we can for the betterment of our children and their future. Too many people are looking for excuses, handouts, and someone to blame their problems on. Instead, they should look to themselves, accept the situation they're in, and decide to make the best of it. When you focus on yourself and take a look at what you can improve in your own life, then you'll be ready to take action. As we consistently take small steps in pursuit of big dreams, results are inevitable. It's not going to happen overnight (Rome wasn't built in a day!), but when we put our heads down and keep going, the hope for a better future should catapult our present into a better world.

It's not easy to improve. It takes the humility to accept that we can be better and the courage to work toward our goals. When we make the decision to be a better version of ourselves, we must be committed. It's not a one-stop shop. The world provides many opportunities to rationalize laziness and mediocrity, it's full of people who settle for average. But as we take the necessary steps to improve ourselves, our perceptions slowly begin leaning in a more positive direction.

Pointing fingers and complaining is a result of passive negligence and solves nothing. If you believe things can get better, they will. It's not easy. It's a daily battle, but if you stick to your guns and push through the tough times, eventually you'll see results, perceptions will change, and your world can slowly teeter back to a land of opportunity instead of a prison of stress, obligation, mixed in with brief moments of happiness.

The aim of this book is to encourage adults to make the greatest impact in their world as possible. For those willing to take an honest look at their current situation in life and the world around them with a willingness to do the necessary work to achieve excellence, the possibilities are endless. Hopefully, these pages have inspired individuals to turn inwards and objectively assess their strengths, weaknesses, desires, and overall health and well-being for the purpose of manifesting their deepest passions while inspiring others toward the same.

The key to fulfillment and accomplishing our dreams isn't somewhere "out there" among the stars. We've all been designed with unique talents, and if we would stop for a moment and take a long, deep look within, we could then discover our personal truth and natural abilities, while also accepting our selfish inclinations toward procrastination. Most people are distracted by daily obligations and never take the time to ask themselves who they really are and what they really want out of life. If one does contemplate his dreams, it's even rarer that he'll go to task toward making them a reality.

It's natural to seek comfort in life, but in that pursuit lies the root of all lack in our lives. Once we think we've found our "role" in life, it's tempting to tap the brakes and think that we've made it. However, what truth seekers come to realize is that in the pursuit of goals lies the fulfillment we're searching for. Once we reach the mountaintop of our imaginations, we realize that our initial goal was only the beginning. As we live and learn, we realize that the pursuit is an ongoing journey where searching, growing, and pushing ourselves to greater heights is the key to fulfillment, not the destination itself.

These pages are not only for teachers and parents but for anyone who wants to thrive in whatever arena they're a part of. If we want the world to improve, we need to first focus on ourselves so that we can have the clarity to inspire others. Parents and teachers both have a shared responsibility to positively impact the lives of children. Their world is shaped by those in charge of their care. Children are the future, but we're the ones in charge of setting the stage. Will you lead them to greener pastures or set up barriers that thwart their potential? It's up to adults to lead, but in order to do so, we must take charge of ourselves. So the next time you see a young person, understand you have the power of inspiration, and they're watching.

ABOUT THE AUTHOR

The experience teaching in the inner city of Dallas gave the author, Jackson Reap, a passion to go beyond the confines of the classroom in pursuit of making a difference in people's lives. After earning a Bachelor's degree in Psychology from the University of North Texas, Reap decided to go into an area where luxuries like psychologists weren't readily available to most parents.

Teaching has provided Reap the opportunity to gain insights into the hectic realities facing children today, as well as the limitations burdening teachers. *The Future is Watching* was written in hopes of inspiring not only teachers and parents but anyone hoping to impact future generations.

Lightning Source UK Ltd.
Milton Keynes UK
UKHW041053050720
365993UK00002BA/406